Delicious

VEGETABLES

with

HERBS

DAWN J. RANCK and
PHYLLIS PELLMAN GOOD

Good Books

Intercourse, PA 17534

Cover design and illustration by Cheryl Benner
Design by Dawn J. Ranck
Illustrations by Cheryl Benner

DELICIOUSLY EASY VEGETABLES WITH HERBS
Copyright © 1998 by Good Books, Intercourse, Pennsylvania, 17534
International Standard Book Number: 1-56148-257-9
Library of Congress Catalog Card Number: 98-41852

Library of Congress Cataloging-in-Publication Data
Ranck, Dawn J.
    Deliciously easy vegetables with herbs / Dawn J. Ranck and
Phyllis Pellman Good.
        p. cm. -- (Deliciously easy -- with herbs)
    ISBN 1-56148-257-9
    1. Cookery (Vegetables) 2. Cookers (Herbs) I. Good,
Phyllis Pellman. II. Title. III. Series: Ranck, Dawn J.
Deliciously easy -- with herbs.
TX801.R35 1998
641.6'5--dc21   98-41852
                                                                      CIP

Table of Contents

Green Beans with Parsley and Mint

Diane Clement
Clement Herb Farm
Rogers, AR

Makes 6 servings

1½ lbs. fresh green beans
¼ cup extra virgin olive oil
3 Tbps. chopped fresh mint
  (3 tsp. dried)
3 Tbsp. chopped fresh
  parsley (3 tsp. dried)

salt to taste
freshly ground black pepper
  to taste
2 Tbsp. fresh lemon juice
4 tsp. grated lemon peel

1. Cook beans in salt water until tender. Drain. Refresh in bowl of ice water. Drain well.
2. Mix together oil, mint, parsley, salt, and pepper. Pour over beans. Toss.
3. Just before serving, mix in lemon juice and lemon peel. Serve at room temperature.

Great Green Beans

Carol Frank
Summer Kitchen Herbs
Allenton, WI

Makes 4 servings

1 quart fresh green beans
3 6" branches summer savory
3 sprigs parsley

1 clove garlic, minced
2 Tbsp. butter or olive oil

1. Cook beans in salt water until crisp-tender.
2. Strip leaves off stems of savory. Cut leaves off parsley. Chop herbs as fine as possible.
3. Drain beans. Toss with herbs, garlic, and butter or oil. Serve immediately.

Lima Beans Catalance

Judy Keas
Cricket Hill Herb Farm
Rowley, MA

Makes 4 servings

4 Tbsp. butter
1 cup bacon bits
16-oz. pkg. frozen lima beans or
  1 lb. parboiled fresh limas
¼ cup onion, chopped
1 clove garlic, minced
1 bay leaf

1 tsp. chopped fresh mint
  (⅓ tsp. dried)
2 tsp. chopped fresh
  parsley (⅔ tsp. dried)
¼ cup cooking sherry
1 cup chunks of cooked
  sausage

1. Saute bacon bits in butter. Remove bacon bits and add lima beans. Cover and cook on low heat for 10 minutes.
2. Add onion, garlic, bay leaf, mint, and parsley. Cover and cook on low heat for 5 minutes.
3. Stir in sherry. Cover and cook for 10 minutes.
4. Add sausage, mixing well. Cook uncovered for several minutes until beans are tender.
5. Serve garnished with bacon bits.

White Bean Casserole

Jennifer Lommen
Passion Flower Nursery
Christiansburg, VA

Makes 6-8 servings

2 cups dried white beans	1 Tbsp. fresh thyme
4 medium onions, chopped	(1 tsp. dried)
or sliced thin	1 tsp. olive oil
2 Tbsp. fresh basil, chopped	salt and pepper to taste
(1 Tbsp. dried)	4 slices toasted bread
2 Tbsp. fresh parsley, chopped	1 Tbsp. olive oil
(1 Tbsp. dried)	2 Tbsp. butter or margarine

1. Soak beans overnight in 8 cups water; then cook until soft, approximately 2 to 3 hours.
2. Saute onions and herbs in 1 tsp. olive oil.
3. Mix together tender beans and sauteed onions and herbs. Place in greased casserole.
4. Blend bread and 1 Tbsp. olive oil in food processor. Sprinkle bread crumbs over vegetables.
5. Place chunks of butter or margarine over top.
6. Bake at 350° for 20-30 minutes.

Basil Refried Beans

Jacqueline Swift
Rainbow's End Herbs
Perrysburg, NY

Makes 6-8 servings

1 Tbsp. vegetable oil	2 Tbsp. chopped fresh basil
1 Tbsp. butter or margarine	(2 tsp. dried)
1 1/2 cups diced onion	1 1/2 tsp. chopped fresh
2 cloves garlic, minced	rosemary (1/2 tsp. dried)
3 cups cooked pinto beans	pinch cayenne pepper
(any brown or red bean	salt to taste
will do)	1/2 cup cheddar cheese
1 tsp. cumin	

1. Saute onion and garlic in oil and butter for 10 minutes.
2. Add beans, cumin, basil, rosemary, pepper, and salt. Cook for 15 minutes.
3. Remove half of beans and mash or chop in blender. Stir in cheese until melted.
4. Mix together both bean mixtures and serve.

Broccoli Corn Casserole

Gerry Bauman
The Farmhouse
Grimes, IA

Makes 6 servings

10 oz. frozen chopped
  broccoli, thawed
2 cups cream-style corn
1/2 cup cracker crumbs
1 egg, beaten
1/2 tsp. salt
1 1/2 tsp. chopped fresh
  rosemary (1/2 tsp. dried)

1 1/2 tsp. chopped fresh
  thyme (1/2 tsp. dried)
1/2 cup cracker crumbs
1 Tbsp. minced onion
dash of pepper
2 Tbsp. butter
4 slices chopped,
  cooked bacon

1. Combine broccoli, corn, 1/2 cup cracker crumbs, egg, salt, rosemary, and thyme in greased casserole dish.
2. Mix together 1/2 cup cracker crumbs, onion, pepper, and butter. Spread over casserole. Top with bacon.
3. Bake at 350° for 45 minutes.

Harvard Beets with Dill

Dorothy Weaver & Pat Dyer
Village Herb Shop
Blue Ball, PA

Makes 4-6 servings

2 16-oz. cans beets, drained
1/3 cup sugar
2 Tbsp. flour
1/4 cup water

1/4 cup dill vinegar
1 1/2 Tbsp. chopped fresh
dill (1/2 Tbsp. dried)

1. Place beets in crockpot.
2. Mix together sugar and flour. Stir in water and vinegar, blending until smooth. Pour over beets.
3. Cover and cook on high for 3-4 hours, stirring once each hour.
4. Sprinkle with dill leaves before serving.

Broccoli with Capers

Mary Clair Wenger
Sassafras Hill Herbs
Kimmswick, MO

Makes 6 servings

1 large head of broccoli,
     or 24-oz. frozen broccoli
1/4 cup butter
1/8 tsp. ground black pepper
2 tsp. capers
1 1/2 tsp. chopped fresh
     oregano (1/2 tsp. dried)

1. Steam broccoli. Keep warm.
2. Melt butter in saucepan. Stir in pepper, capers, and oregano. Mix well.
3. Pour over broccoli. Serve.

Minted Carrots

Sandie Shores
Herb's Herbs and such . . .
Rochester, MN

Makes 4-6 servings

1¹/₂ lbs. young carrots
¹/₄ cup butter
1 heaping Tbsp. sugar

2 Tbsp. chopped fresh
spearmint (2 tsp. dried)

1. Cut carrots into quarters, slices, or julienne strips. Steam until tender. Drain.
2. Slowly melt butter in saucepan. Stir in sugar. Stir over low heat for 3-4 minutes until the mixture is faintly caramelized. Cover and let stand for 2 minutes.
3. Stir in chopped mint.
4. Add carrots and coat well.

Note: If using dried mint, add after butter is melted in Step 2.

Rosemary Glazed Carrots

Nancy Ketner
Sweet Earth
West Reading, PA

Makes 3-4 servings

12 carrots, peeled and sliced
¹/₄-¹/₃ cup rosemary honey *
3 Tbsp. butter

1 tsp. fresh rosemary
(¹/₃ tsp. dried)

1. Cook carrots until tender but firm.
2. Mix together honey and butter until butter is melted.
3. Drain carrots. Toss in honey mixture. Sprinkle with rosemary.

*** Rosemary Honey**
Steep several sprigs of fresh rosemary in a light flavored honey for a week or more.

Carrots Tarragon

Irene L. Weidenbacher
Herbs in the Woods
Hollidaysburg, PA

Makes 4 servings

6 large carrots, peeled and
   cut into 3"-long strips
2 Tbsp. butter

1/4 tsp. white pepper
3 Tbsp. chopped fresh
   tarragon (1 tsp. dried)

1. Steam carrots until tender.
2. While carrots are cooking, melt butter in saucepan. Add tarragon and white pepper and simmer at low temperature.
3. Drain carrots. Add butter and tarragon. Toss and serve.

Grilled Eggplant

Linda E. Sampson Costa
Sampson's Herb Farm
East Bridgewater, MA

Makes 2 servings

large sprig fresh rosemary
1/2 cup extra virgin olive oil
2 small, homegrown eggplants

1. Mix together rosemary and olive oil. Let stand for 15 minutes.
2. Cut eggplant into 1/4" slices.
3. Brush each slice with oil and grill for 3-5 minutes on each side, until nicely browned.

Herb Mushrooms on the Grill

Irene L. Weidenbacher
Herbs in the Woods
Hollidaysburg, PA

Makes 4 servings

8 large mushrooms, whole or sliced	3 tsp. chopped fresh thyme (1 tsp. dried)
2 Tbsp. butter	3 tsp. chopped fresh summer savory
3 tsp. chopped fresh oregano (1 tsp. dried)	(1 tsp. dried) (optional)

1. Make a pocket out of aluminum foil.
2. Place mushrooms, butter, and herbs in foil. Fold tightly to seal.
3. Place mushrooms on grill. Shake every 5 minutes to avoid burning. Grill for approximately 20 minutes.

Mediterranean Onions

Barbara Warren
Provincial Herbs
Folsom, PA

Makes 4-6 servings

4 medium onions	1 Tbsp. chopped fresh thyme (1 tsp. dried)
1/2 tsp. pepper	1 tsp. butter
dash of saffron or turmeric	1 tsp. olive oil
1 Tbsp. chopped fresh parsley (1 tsp. dried)	
1 Tbsp. chopped fresh chives (1 tsp. dried)	

1. Cut onions into 1/4" thick slices. Separate into rings.
2. Combine onions, pepper, saffron, parsley, chives, and thyme.
3. Melt butter in large skillet. Add olive oil and onions. Cook for 25 minutes, or until onions are tender and brown.

Herb Peas

Betty Summers
Herbs 'n Things
Muskogee, OK

Makes 4-6 servings

1 lb. small peas
1 Tbsp. chopped fresh chives
  (1 tsp. dried)
dash of white wine

1 Tbsp. chopped fresh sweet
  marjoram (1 tsp. dried)
sprinkle of nutmeg

In saucepan, mix together all ingredients. Bring to a boil and simmer for about 1 minute.

Braised Peas with Mint

Anna L. Brown
Longfellow's Greenhouses
Manchester, ME

Makes 4 servings

2 tsp. vegetable oil
1 tsp. finely minced ginger
  (optional)
2 scallions, white part only,
  finely chopped
1 Tbsp. chopped fresh mint
  leaves (1 tsp. dried)
2 cups fresh or frozen peas

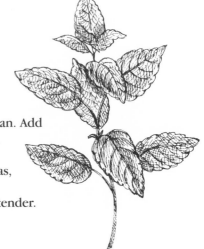

1. Heat oil in medium saucepan. Add ginger, scallions, and mint. Stir-fry briefly.
2. Add peas (if using fresh peas, add 2 Tbsp. water).
3. Cover and simmer just till tender.

Mint-Liscious Peas

Carol Lacko-Beem

Herbs-Liscious

Marshalltown, IA

Makes 4 servings

16-oz. pkg. frozen peas
2 tsp. chopped onion
1 small garlic clove, minced
3 Tbsp. thinly sliced or diced
   sweet red pepper (optional)
pinch of Hungarian paprika

1½ tsp. chopped fresh mint
   (½ tsp. cut and
   sifted dried)
1 Tbsp. butter
3 Tbsp. chicken broth

1. Cook peas, onion, garlic, and sweet pepper in small amount of water until just tender.
2. Stir in remaining ingredients. Mix well. Return to heat until butter is melted.
3. Serve immediately.

Herb Roasted Potatoes

Nancy Raleigh

HBB

Belcamp, MD

Makes 6-8 servings

3 lbs. new potatoes, cut in half
3 Tbsp. olive oil
1 Tbsp. chopped fresh thyme
   (1 tsp. dried)
1 Tbsp. chopped fresh rosemary
   (1 tsp. dried)

1 tsp. coarse salt
½ tsp. black crushed
   peppercorns
minced fresh herbs for
   garnish

1. Combine all ingredients except herbs for garnish. Toss well.
2. Arrange in single layer in baking pan.
3. Roast at 400° for 20 minutes. Turn and roast for 15-20 minutes, or until tender and golden.
4. Top with fresh herbs and serve.

Garlic-Thyme Oven Roasted Potatoes

Linda Hangren
LinHaven Gardens
Omaha, NE

Makes 6 servings

3 Tbsp. olive oil
6 large potatoes, peeled
   and cut in 1" pieces
3 cloves garlic

1½ Tbsp. chopped fresh
   thyme, lemon thyme,
   or dill (1½ tsp. dried)

1. Pour olive oil in bottom of 9" x 13" pan.
2. Stir in potatoes and garlic. Stir to coat with oil.
3. Bake at 400° for 25 minutes. Remove from oven. Sprinkle with thyme and stir well.
4. Bake at 350° for 30-40 minutes, or until potatoes are tender.

Herbed Potatoes

Kelly Wisner
Herbal Heaven
Wernersville, PA

Makes 3-4 servings

4 new red potatoes,
   cut in bite-sized pieces
2 tsp. oil
1½ tsp. chopped fresh sage
   (½ tsp. dried)

1½ tsp. chopped fresh
   rosemary (½ tsp. dried)
4 tsp. chopped fresh parsley
   (1⅓ tsp. dried)

1. Mix together potatoes and oil. Stir to coat. Place in baking pan.
2. Bake at 350° for 30 minutes.
3. Sprinkle with sage, rosemary, and parsley. Serve.

Polish Potatoes

Mary "Auntie M" Mizio Embler
Auntie M's Enchanted Garden
Clayton, NC

Makes 4-6 servings

¹/₂ cup butter
2 Tbsp. chopped fresh chives
  (2 tsp. dried)
2 Tbsp. chopped fresh parsley
  (2 tsp. dried)
3 Tbsp. chopped fresh dill
  (1 Tbsp. dried)

1 lb. potatoes,
  boiled and cut into
  bite-sized pieces
salt to taste
pepper to taste

1. In saucepan, mix together butter, chives, parsley, and dill.
2. Add potatoes and saute until heated through.
3. Salt and pepper to taste.

Fabulous Fingerlings

Carol Turner
Turkey Trot Trunk
Mountain City, GA

Makes 6 servings

1 lb. potatoes
  (fingerlings are preferred)
1 tsp. salt
4 Tbsp. butter
1 Tbsp. olive oil

6 Tbsp. chopped fresh
  parsley (2 Tbsp. dried)
6 Tbsp. chopped fresh chives
  (2 Tbsp. dried)

1. Cook potatoes and salt in large pot for 20-25 minutes, until tender. Drain.
2. Mix together butter, oil, parsley, and chives. Pour over potatoes. Toss until well coated. Serve immediately.

Variations: Use any of these herb combinations, in place of the parsley and chives: lovage and sage, rosemary and parsley, tarragon and chives, oregano and paprika.

Herbed Sliced Baked Potatoes

Louise Hyde
Well-Sweep Herb Farm
Port Murray, NJ

Makes 4 servings

4 medium potatoes
2 Tbsp. butter, melted
3 Tbsp. chopped fresh herbs:
savory, thyme, chives,
and/or rosemary
(or use 3 tsp. assorted dried)

4 Tbsp. grated
cheddar cheese
2 Tbsp. Parmesan cheese

1. Cut potatoes into thin even slices from top to bottom, being careful not to cut all the way through the bottom of the potatoes. Put potatoes in backing dish, fanning the slices slightly.
2. Drizzle with butter. Sprinkle with herbs, making sure to get them between the slices.
3. Bake at 425° for 45 minutes, or until done. Remove from oven.
4. Sprinkle with cheese. Return to oven until cheese is melted.

Dill Potatoes

Jane D. Look
Pineapple Hill Herbs & More
Mapleton, IL

Makes 6 servings

6-8 potatoes, cut in half
1 tsp. salt
4 sprigs fresh dill
(2 tsp. dried)

3 Tbsp. butter
3 Tbsp. chopped fresh dill
(3 tsp. dried)

1. Place potatoes in pan. Cover with water.
2. Add salt and sprigs of dill. Bring to boil. Reduce heat and simmer for 20-30 minutes, or until potatoes are soft. Drain water and discard dill sprigs.
3. Mix together butter and chopped dill. Pour over potatoes and serve.

Lemon Oregano Potatoes

Mary Ellen Warchol
Stockbridge Herbs & Stitches
South Deerfield, MA

Makes 6 servings

2 Tbsp. butter
4 lbs. Idaho potatoes,
    peeled and cut into
    1¹/₂" chunks
¹/₃ cup chopped fresh oregano
    (5 tsp. dried)

salt to taste
pepper to taste
¹/₂ cup lemon juice
¹/₂ cup olive or vegetable oil

1. Melt butter in bottom of 9" x 13" baking pan.
2. In large mixing bowl, toss together potatoes, oregano, salt, pepper, lemon juice, and oil. Return to baking pan and spread in single layer.
3. Add water to cover the potatoes about ¹/₃ of the way up.
4. Bake at 400° for about 45 minutes, or until potatoes are golden brown and soft.

Rosemary Roast Potatoes

Doris Delatte
Homestead Horticulture
Elk, WA

Makes 4 servings

¼ cup olive oil
2 cloves garlic, minced
1 Tbsp. chopped fresh rosemary
   (1 tsp. dried)
salt to taste

2 lbs. potatoes,
   cut in large chunks
chives or garlic chives
   for garnish

1. Mix together oil, garlic, rosemary, and salt.
2. Roll potatoes in herb oil until coated. Transfer to shallow baking dish. Pour any remaining oil over potatoes.
3. Bake at 400° for 45 minutes, or until potatoes are tender and brown. Garnish with finely chopped chives.

Rosemary Potatoes

Madeline Wajda
Willow Pond Farm
Fairfield, PA

Makes 8 servings

8 large potatoes
½ cup olive oil
4 large garlic cloves, minced
salt to taste

pepper to taste
3 Tbsp. chopped fresh
   rosemary (1 Tbsp. dried)

1. Cut each potato into 8 spears.
2. Toss together potatoes, oil, garlic, salt, and pepper. Marinate at room temperature for 30 minutes.
3. Spread potatoes on baking sheet.
4. Bake at 350° for 45 minutes, tossing occasionally.
5. Sprinkle with rosemary and continue roasting until potatoes are crusty brown, about 15-20 minutes.

Rosemary Pan-Fried Potatoes

Linda Jani and Chris Aylesworth
Viewhurst Farm Herb and Garden Shop
Hebron, IN

Makes 6 servings

4 medium red potatoes,
   unpeeled but cubed
2 Tbsp. olive oil

2 Tbsp. chopped fresh
   rosemary (2 tsp. dried)
salt to taste

1. In non-stick pan, saute potatoes in oil until tender.
2. Add rosemary and salt during last 2-3 minutes of cooking.

Oven-Fried Rosemary Potatoes

Connie Slagle
Rustic Garden Herbs
Roann, IN
Jim O'Toole
Madison, FL

Makes 4 servings

2 lbs. russet potatoes,
   cut in 1/4" slices
1/2 cup olive oil
1 1/2 tsp. salt
freshly ground coarse
   black pepper

handful of fresh rosemary
   sprigs, 1 1/2-2" long
3-4 cloves of garlic

1. Dredge both sides of potato slices in oil.
2. Place in slightly oiled 9" x 13" baking dish and sprinkle with salt and pepper.
3. Lay 1 or 2 rosemary sprigs on each potato slice. Fill in all the empty spaces between potato slices with sliced garlic cloves.
4. Cover and bake at 400° for 20-25 minutes. Remove cover, and turn potatoes over with a metal turner. Bake for an additional 20 minutes, or until potatoes are tender and golden brown.
5. Drain any excess oil and move potatoes onto serving platter, turning potatoes so their rosemary sides are up.

Potato Slices with Rosemary and Cheese

Mary Ellen Wilcox
SouthRidge Treasures Herb Shop
Scotia, NY

Makes 4 servings

4 medium-sized potatoes,
  unpeeled and sliced
2 tsp. vegetable oil
1 Tbsp. chopped fresh
  rosemary (1 tsp. dried)

1/4 tsp. paprika
3/4 cup shredded cheddar
  cheese with jalapeno
  peppers, or Monterey
  Jack cheese with jalapeno
  peppers

1. Place potatoes in shallow microwave-safe baking dish. Brush with oil.
2. Sprinkle with rosemary and paprika. Stir to coat potatoes. Cover with waxed paper.
3. Microwave on High for 10-12 minutes, stirring twice, until potatoes are almost tender.
4. Sprinkle with cheese. Cover and let stand for 5 minutes, until cheese is melted and potatoes are tender.

Hot Potato Salad

Elaine Seibel
Scents and Non Scents
Hill, NH

Makes 4 servings

1 1/2 lbs. small new potatoes,
  cut in chunks
1 Tbsp. vegetable oil
4 cloves garlic, minced
4 sprigs fresh rosemary

1 Tbsp. herbal vinegar
2 Tbsp. Dijon-style mustard
1/4 tsp. black pepper
2 green onions, sliced

1. Combine potatoes with oil. Place in roasting pan. Top with garlic and sprigs of rosemary.
2. Bake at 400° for 30 minutes, stirring often.
3. Whisk together vinegar, mustard, pepper, and onions.
4. Pour over hot potoates. Stir and serve warm.

Sage Potatoes

Linda E. Sampson Costa
Sampson's Herb Farm
East Bridgewater, MA

Makes 4 servings

4-6 Red Bliss or new potatoes,
cut in bite-sized pieces
1 tsp. finely chopped fresh sage

2 Tbsp. butter
salt to taste
freshly ground pepper
to taste

1. Simmer potatoes in salt water until tender. Drain.
2. Add sage, butter, salt, and pepper. Toss well and serve.

Creamy Potatoes

Karen Ashworth
The Herb Shoppe
Duenweg, MO

Makes 8 servings

8 medium-sized potatoes,
sliced thin
2/3 cup chopped bell pepper
1/2 cup chopped fresh parsley
(2 1/2 Tbsp. dried)
6 Tbsp. minced scallions

2 Tbsp. grated fresh
Parmesan cheese
4 Tbsp. cornstarch
3 Tbsp. margarine
dash of pepper
3 cups milk

1. Put thin layer of potatoes on bottom of greased baking dish.
2. Mix together pepper, parsley, scallions, cheese, and cornstarch.
   Pour half of mixture over potatoes. Dot with margarine.
   Repeat layers.
3. Season with pepper, and pour milk over top. Cover.
4. Bake at 350° for 90 minutes, or until done.

Herbed Potato Pie

Georgia Pomphrey
Full Circle Farm
Rockford, TN

Makes 8 servings

6-8 medium-sized potatoes
1 cup cottage cheese
1¹/2 cups shredded sharp
  cheddar cheese
7 eggs
2 small green onions, chopped
  (include stems)
4 drops hot sauce
³/4 tsp. salt

dash of pepper
³/4 tsp. chopped fresh
  oregano (¹/4 tsp. dried)
³/4 tsp. chopped fresh
  thyme (¹/4 tsp. dried)
³/4 tsp. chopped fresh
  marjoram (¹/4 tsp. dried)
³/4 tsp. chopped fresh chives
  (¹/4 tsp. dried)

1. Cook potatoes until soft. Cool, peel, and grate.
2. Add remaining ingredients to grated potatoes. Stir well.
3. Pour into greased 9" x 13" casserole dish. Refrigerate for at least 8 hours.
4. Bake at 350° for 30 minutes, or until firm. Cut into squares and serve.

Baked Stuffed Potatoes

Elaine Seibel
Scents and Non-Scents
Hill, NH

Makes 4 servings

4 baking potatoes
²/3 cup sour cream
3 Tbsp. chopped fresh parsley
  (1 Tbsp. dried)
2 Tbsp. chopped fresh dill
  (2 tsp. dried)

1 Tbsp. chopped fresh chives
  (1 tsp. dried)
paprika to taste

1. Bake potatoes at 400° for 45-60 minutes, or until soft. Remove from oven. Cut in half lengthwise.

2. With spoon, scoop out potato, leaving shell intact.
3. Mix together hot potatoes, sour cream, and herbs. Mash until smooth and creamy. Spoon mixture back into potato skins. Sprinkle with paprika.
4. Place on baking sheet. Bake at 400° for 25 minutes, or until piping hot.

Note: These freeze well. After stuffing potato skins, place on cookie sheet or in a flat container, cover, and freeze. Before serving, bake at 400° for 30 minutes, or until heated through.

Potato Herb Stuffing

Lewis J. Matt III
White Buck Farm
Holbrook, PA

Makes 8 servings

4 celery stalks with leaves, chopped
1 large onion, chopped
1 clove garlic, minced
4 large potatoes, cooked and diced
1/4 lb. butter or margarine
1 quart vegetable or meat broth
6 eggs
10 slices whole wheat bread, diced

1/2 cup chopped fresh parsley (2 1/2 Tbsp. dried)
1 Tbsp. chopped fresh basil (1 tsp. dried)
1 1/2 tsp. chopped fresh thyme (1/2 tsp. dried)
1 1/2 tsp. chopped fresh lemon thyme (1/2 tsp. dried)
1 tsp. freshly ground pepper
3/4 tsp. salt
water

1. Saute celery, onion, garlic, and potatoes in butter. Cover with lid and steam until tender.
2. Beat together broth and eggs. Add bread, herbs, pepper, and salt. Mix completely.
3. Stir in celery mixture. If not moist, add water and stir in gently.
4. Press mixture into greased casserole dish.
5. Cover and bake at 350° for 1 hour. Uncover and bake until top begins to brown.
6. Serve with any gravy, or allow to cool and slice and serve cold. Excellent with currant or cranberry jelly, chutney, or relish.

Bean and Potato Thyme

Lucy Scanlon
Merrymount Herbs
Norris, TN

Makes 4 servings

3 cups water
3 tsp. instant bouillon
8 onions, 1" in diameter*
12 small new potatoes,
    1" in diameter *
1½ tsp. chopped fresh
    rosemary (½ tsp. dried)
3 cups snap beans,
    cut in 1" pieces

8 medium mushrooms,
    sliced
1½ Tbsp. chopped fresh
    thyme (½ Tbsp. dried)
melted butter or margarine
freshly ground black pepper
    to taste

1. Boil together water and bouillon. Reduce heat
   slightly. Add onions and simmer for 4 minutes.
2. Stir in potatoes and rosemary. Simmer about
   10 minutes more, or until onions and potatoes are almost soft.
3. Stir in green beans, mushrooms, and
   thyme. Continue gentle simmer until beans
   are crisp-tender.
4. Drain liquid. Stir butter or margarine into
   vegetables. Grind pepper over top.

*Or use large-sized potatoes and
onions and cut them in 1" cubes.*

Pan Roasted Vegetables with Rosemary & Garlic Chives

Ary Bruno
Koinonia Farm
Stevenson, MD

Makes 6-8 servings

1½ lbs. small, new potatoes, cut in half
3-4 Tbsp. olive oil
¼ cup water
1 lb. small zucchini or other green summer squash, 4"-6" long
1 sweet red bell pepper, cored and cut in ¼"-wide strips
1 lb. eggplant, peeled and sliced thin*
4 Tbsp. chopped fresh garlic chives (4 tsp. dried), or 3 Tbsp. fresh chives (1 Tbsp. dried), plus 1 garlic clove, minced

1 Tbsp. minced fresh rosemary (1 tsp. dried)
16-oz. can chickpeas, drained and rinsed
pinch of sugar
sea salt to taste
black pepper to taste
¼ cup water
½ cup grated fresh Parmesan cheese

1. Saute potates in oil for 2-3 minutes. Add ¼ cup water and cover. Cook until water is mostly evaporated, about 8-10 minutes.
2. Cut zucchini in matchstick-sized strips. Add to potatoes, along with pepper, eggplant, and garlic. Saute until brown.
3. Stir in rosemary, chickpeas, sugar, salt, and pepper. Add ¼ cup water. Cook about 4 minutes, or until vegetables are tender, stirring occasionally.
4. Serve with Parmesan cheese.

If using regular, dark purple or Japanese eggplant, slice it 30 minutes before cooking time and soak it in salt water to remove its bitterness. Squeeze gently to remove excess water before sauteing.

Vegetable Stir-Fry

Karen Ashworth
The Herb Shoppe
Duenweg, MO

Makes 4 servings

1 cup red onions, chopped	1/4 tsp. cumin
1 cup carrots, cut in pieces	2 Tbsp. margarine
1 cup broccoli, cut in pieces	1/2 cup almonds, blanched
1 cup cauliflower, cut in pieces	and chopped
2 garlic cloves, minced	1/4 cup sunflower seeds
1 1/2 tsp. fresh basil	2 Tbsp. soy sauce
(1/2 tsp. dried)	

1. Saute vegetables, garlic, basil, and cumin in margarine for 5 minutes.
2. Stir in almonds. Cover and cook 3 minutes.
3. Add sunflower seeds and soy sauce. Stir. Cover. Cook 2 minutes.
4. Serve over rice or any other cooked grains.

Roasted Vegetables

Nancy Raleigh
HBB
Belcamp, MD

Makes 8 servings

4 large potatoes, unpeeled, cut in chunks	2 large red peppers, cut into chunks
1 medium-sized onion, cut in wedges	2 large yellow peppers, cut into chunks
3 Tbsp. vegetable oil	1 Tbsp. chopped fresh thyme (1 tsp. dried)
1/2 tsp. salt	1 1/2 tsp. chopped fresh basil (1/2 tsp. dried)
bunch of baby carrots	
pattypan or yellow neck squash, cut into chunks	1/2 tsp. ground pepper
1/2 lb. green beans	1 large lemon, thinly sliced

1. In large roasting pan, toss potatoes, onion, oil, and salt.
2. Roast at 425° for 15 minutes.
3. Add carrots, squash, beans, peppers, thyme, basil, black pepper, and half the lemon slices.
4. Return to oven and roast for 45 minutes, turning occasionally.
5. Arrange vegetables on platter and garnish with remaining lemon slices.

Note: Use any mix of vegetables. Sweet potatoes are also good.

Summer Veggie Bake

Eone Riales
Fogg Road Herb Farm
Nesbit, MS

Makes 8-10 servings

6 Tbsp. butter
3 medium-sized yellow
   squash, trimmed and
   sliced thin
10 oz. fresh spinach,
   washed and trimmed
3 medium-sized tomatoes,
   sliced

1 cup cream-style
   cottage cheese
1½ cups saltine cracker
   crumbs
3 tsp. chopped fresh lemon
   thyme (1 tsp. dried)
3 slices cheese, cut into
   strips

1. Saute squash in 2 Tbsp. butter. Set aside.
2. Saute spinach lightly in 2 Tbsp. butter. Set aside.
3. Saute tomatoes lightly in 2 Tbsp. butter. Set aside.
4. Mix together cottage cheese, cracker crumbs, and thyme in small bowl.
5. Place squash in shallow baking dish. Cover with half of cottage cheese mixture. Place spinach on top. Cover with remaining cottage cheese mixture. Top with sliced tomatoes. Arrange cheese strips over tomatoes in crisscross fashion.
6. Bake at 350° for 30 minutes.

Baked Lentils with Cheese

Jan Mast
The Herb Shop
Lititz, PA

Makes 6 servings

1³/₄ cups lentils, rinsed
2 cups water
1 bay leaf
2 tsp. salt
¹/₄ tsp. pepper
¹/₂ tsp. chopped fresh marjoram
  (¹/₈ tsp. dried)
¹/₂ tsp. chopped fresh sage
  (¹/₈ tsp. dried)
¹/₂ tsp. chopped fresh thyme
  (¹/₈ tsp. dried)

2 large onions, chopped
2 garlic cloves, minced
2 cups canned tomatoes
2 large carrots, sliced
  ¹/₈" thick
¹/₂ cup thinly sliced celery
1 green pepper, chopped
2 Tbsp. parsley
3 cups shredded cheddar
  cheese

1. Combine lentils, water, bay leaf, salt, pepper, marjoram, sage, thyme, onions, cloves, and tomatoes in 9" x 13" baking dish. Cover tightly.
2. Bake at 375° for 30 minutes.
3. Uncover and stir in carrots and celery. Cover and bake for 40 minutes.
4. Stir in green pepper and parsley. Sprinkle cheese on top. Bake, uncovered, for 5 minutes, or until cheese melts.

Herbed Tomato Bake

Leslie Scott
Once Upon a Thyme
Troy, NY

Makes 6 servings

3 medium-sized tomatoes
margarine or butter
1¹/₂ tsp. chopped fresh basil
1¹/₂ tsp. chopped fresh oregano
1¹/₂ tsp. chopped fresh parsley
1¹/₄ cups grated Parmesan cheese

³/₄ cup fine-crumb bread
  crumbs
salt to taste
pepper to taste

1. Cut tomatoes in half around the middle. Place in baking dish, skin side down. Cut small slits across the top of each tomato, without cutting through the skin, to allow ingredients to bake in.
2. Place a chunk of margarine on each half.
3. Mix together herbs, Parmesan cheese, and bread crumbs. Sprinkle herb mix, salt, and pepper on each tomato.
4. Bake at 325° for 20-25 minutes.

Spaghetti Squash Primavera

Shari Jensen
Naturalicious Products
Fountain, CO

Makes 4 servings

1 medium spaghetti squash
2 medium carrots, diced
2 cups broccoli florets
2 cups quartered mushrooms
1 medium zucchini, diced
1/2 cup chopped green onion
1 Tbsp. olive oil
2 cups peeled, seeded, and diced Roma or beefsteak tomatoes

1/2 cup chopped fresh basil leaves (3 Tbsp. dried)
1/2 cup chopped fresh parsley (3 Tbsp. dried)
4 Tbsp. grated fresh Parmesan cheese
1 clove garlic, minced
1 tsp. salt
pepper to taste

1. Prick skin of squash about 8 times. Place on cookie sheet.
2. Bake at 350° for 90 minutes, or until tender when pierced with fork. Let cool for 20 minutes.
3. Halve lengthwise. Remove seeds. With fork, scrape spaghetti-like strands of squash into a large pan. Set aside.
4. While squash is baking, cook carrots and broccoli until tender. Put in ice water to cool quickly.
5. Saute mushrooms, zucchini, and green onions in 1 Tbsp. olive oil until tender, about 6 minutes.
6. Add squash, carrots, and broccoli. Heat until hot.
7. Combine tomatoes, basil, parsley, Parmesan cheese, garlic, salt, and pepper. Pour over squash mixture. Heat through and serve.

Sauteed Green Tomatoes

Jacoba Baker & Reenie Baker Sandsted
Baker's Acres
Groton, NY

Makes 4 servings

6 medium-sized green tomatoes
1/2 cup flour
salt to taste
pepper to taste
3 Tbsp. butter or bacon drippings

2 1/2 Tbsp. flour
1 cup milk
2 tsp. chopped fresh basil
(2/3 tsp. dried)

1. Slice tomatoes in 1/4" slices. Dredge slices in flour and season with salt and pepper.
2. In skillet, saute tomatoes in butter until browned. Remove to platter and keep warm while making sauce.
3. To make sauce, add flour to skillet and mix well. Cook briefly. Blend in milk, stirring until thickened. Add basil.
4. Pour sauce over tomatoes and serve hot.

Royal Spinach

Jennifer Shadle
The Spice Hunter, Inc.
San Luis Obispo, CA

Makes 3-4 servings

2 Tbsp. butter
4 oz. mushrooms, cleaned
and sliced
1 lb. fresh spinach, cleaned
and drained

1 Tbsp. fresh dill
(1 tsp. dried)
1 Tbsp. sour cream
salt to taste
pepper to taste

1. Saute mushrooms in butter for 3 minutes.
2. Add spinach and stir for 2 minutes.
3. Stir in dill and continue heating for another minute, until spinach is soft and water has evaporated.
4. Remove pan from heat. Fold in sour cream. Mix well. Stir in salt and pepper.

Baked Herb Spinach

Jane D. Look
Pineapple Hill Herbs & More
Mapleton, IL

Makes 4 servings

1 lb. fresh spinach,
   or 10-oz. pkg. frozen spinach
2 eggs, beaten
1/2 cup milk
1 cup grated cheddar cheese
1 cup cooked rice

1/4 cup chopped onion
2 Tbsp. butter or margarine
1/2 tsp. Worcestershire sauce
1 tsp. salt
1 1/2 tsp. chopped fresh
   thyme (1/2 tsp. dried)

1. Cook and drain spinach. Set aside.
2. Combine remaining ingredients. Stir in spinach. Pour into greased casserole dish.
3. Bake at 350° for 20-25 minutes, or until set.

Rice Pilaf

Connie Slagle
Rustic Garden Herbs
Roann, IN

Makes 4 servings

1 Tbsp. chopped fresh sage
   (1 tsp. dried)
1 Tbsp. chopped fresh
   rosemary (1 tsp. dried)
2 Tbsp. chopped fresh
   parsley (2 tsp. dried)

1/2 tsp. garlic powder
1 cup dry rice
2 1/2 cups water
1 Tbsp. butter or margarine

1. Mix together herbs, garlic powder, and dry rice.
2. Add water and butter or margarine. Cover and microwave on High for 5 minutes. Microwave on Power 5 for 15 minutes. Stir and serve.

Herbed Rice

Maria Price-Nowakowski
Willow Oak Flower and Herb Farm
Severn, MD

Makes 4 servings

1¹/₃ cups dry rice
1 Tbsp. olive oil
1 Tbsp. butter or margarine, melted
1 quart hot chicken stock
salt to taste
pepper to taste
3 Tbsp. chopped fresh lemon balm (1 Tbsp. dried)
1 Tbsp. chopped fresh fennel or dill (1 tsp. dried)
1 Tbsp. chopped fresh lemon thyme (1 tsp. dried)
¹/₂ tsp. cinnamon
3 Tbsp. chopped fresh parsley (1 tsp. dried)
¹/₂ tsp. cumin

1. Saute rice in olive oil and butter over medium heat for 5 minutes, stirring constantly. Reduce heat to low and add 1 cup chicken stock. Stir well. Season to taste with salt and pepper.
2. Cook rice, uncovered, over low heat for 18-20 minutes, adding ¹/₂ cup stock every 5 minutes and stirring well at each addition. Continue cooking until rice is al dente and slightly creamy. (It may not be necessary to use all the stock.)
3. Remove from heat and stir in herbs and seasonings. Serve immediately.

About the Authors

Dawn J. Ranck is an advocate of bringing herbs to everyone's kitchens, not just to the cooking artists'.

A resident of Harrisonburg, Virginia, she is also the co-author of *A Quilter's Christmas Cookbook.*

Phyllis Pellman Good, Lancaster, Pennsylvania, has had her hand in many cookbooks—among them, *The Best of Amish Cooking, Recipes from Central Market,* and *The Best of Mennonite Fellowship Meals.*